A Quiz about the
Woman in Your Life

Do You Know Your Bride?

DAN CARLINSKY

 sourcebooks

*Y*ou may think you know almost everything there is to know about the woman you've chosen as your bride. Trust us, this little book will show that really, you don't.

No matter how long you two have known each other, no matter how much you've talked—about matters both serious and foolish—there's plenty you haven't yet learned about her.

This hundred-question quiz will help you to educate yourself, so grab a pencil and see how you do. You won't find the answers in the book, of course. For those, you'll have to check with your bride. When you do, you'll find yourselves talking to each other about each other: your likes and dislikes, your beliefs and opinions, and stories and facts about your pasts.

They're little things, sure, but they aren't insignificant. They're the bits and pieces that make up who we are. And knowing about them is much more than collecting mere personal trivia. Knowing is caring.

Score ten points for each correct answer (taking partial credit wherever you can) and rate yourself according to this scale:

> **Above 900:** What a performance!
>
> **800–900:** Very good for a couple just starting out.
>
> **600–790:** Pretty good. You'll improve as time goes by.
>
> **Below 600:** Ask your bride for a remedial course.

Good luck.

—D.C.

7. **What country, if any, does your bride most want to visit?**

8. **Has she ever gotten seasick?**

____ Yes, once   ____ No

____ Yes, more than once

9. **With people she knows casually, is she better at remembering:**

____ Faces?   ____ Names?

____ Both?   ____ Neither?

10. **Ice cream in a cone or a cup?**

____ Cone   ____ Cup

11. **In a bookstore, which section does she head for first?**

12. **Has she ever thrown something away and then regretted it?**

____ Yes: _____

____ Never

13. Try to name four things your bride never leaves home without.

14. Does she prefer shopping for clothes at:

_____ Bargain stores?   _____ Thrift shops?

_____ Department stores?   _____ Online?

_____ Boutiques?

15. "Money matters should never be discussed in front of the kids." She would:

_____ Agree   _____ Disagree

16. How did she vote in the last big election? (Or did she sit it out?)

17. If you're buying your bride a gift of clothing, what color should you never, ever choose?

18. Of all her friends and relatives, who has a house or apartment she'd move to in a minute?

19. If someone offered you a free weekend on a private island— just you two on the whole place—she'd say:

_____ "Great! When do we go?"

_____ "Uh...you mean we'd be all alone at sea?
With no one around? What if...?"

20. Which older couple does your bride look to as a role model for your marriage?

21. If she has plenty of time, does she prefer:

_____ A bath?   _____ A shower?

22. If served a whole steamed or boiled lobster, would she:

_____ Know how to eat it like a real pro?

_____ Know enough to slog her way through it?

_____ Not know where to start?

23. Who taught her to drive a car?

24. Does she ever eat something straight from the freezer that should be defrosted?

_____ Often   _____ Never

_____ She's done it

25. Is there anyone she hasn't been in touch with for a long time but she'd love to hear from?

_____ Yes: _____

_____ No

26. When nervous, does she:

_____ Munch nonstop?   _____ Close up like a clam?

_____ Not eat a thing?   _____ Fidget, tap, and squirm?

_____ Talk a blue streak?   _____ Bite her nails?

27. If someone at work offers to tell her a raunchy joke, your bride replies:

_____ "Let's hear it."

_____ "I'd rather you didn't."

_____ "Don't bother—I know 'em all."

28. Has she ever gotten an autograph or a signed photo of a celebrity? Does she still own it and know exactly where it is?

_____ Yes, from _____, and it's in

_____.

_____ No

29. Did she keep a diary or journal as a child?

_____ Yes, for a few weeks or months.

_____ Yes, for the better part of a year.

_____ Yes, for a year or more.

_____ She never kept one.

30. Rushing to an important daylong meeting, she notices a tear in her sleeve. Will she:

_____ Go home and change, even though she'll be late?

_____ Get there on time and try to hide the tear all day?

_____ Get there on time and ignore the problem?

_____ Get there on time and explain what happened with a laugh?

31. Would your bride admit to being any of these?

____ Impulsive	____ Passive-aggressive
____ Workaholic	____ Shy
____ Stubborn	____ Gullible
____ Spoiled	____ Petty
____ Easily annoyed	____ A neat freak

32. Has she ever called a radio talk show and appeared on-air? Would she?

____ She has, and she would do it again.

____ She has, but once is enough.

____ She hasn't, but she would.

____ She hasn't, and she wouldn't dream of it.

33. How many of the Three Stooges can she name?

____ Zero	____ Two
____ One	____ Three

34. Can you name at least one summer job or part-time job she had while in school?

35. Did she ever have a crush on a teacher?
(Ten bonus points if you know who.)

_____ Yes: _____ _____

_____ No

36. How does she feel about other people's kids calling her by her first name?

_____ Sure, she prefers it.   _____ Either way is fine with her.

_____ She'd rather they didn't.

37. When was the last time she went to a movie alone?

_____ Within the past month   _____ More than a year ago

_____ Within the past year   _____ Probably never

38. Would she take the last cookie on the plate?

_____ Why not?

_____ Yes, but she'd feel guilty about it.

_____ She just couldn't.

39. "What did the snail say as he rode on the turtle's back?" "Whee!" Your bride will rate this joke:

_____ Hysterically funny.

_____ Silly, but worth a chuckle.

_____ Simply stupid.

40. Which of these scare her?

_____ Thunder and lightning _____ Heights

_____ Snakes _____ Stinging insects

41. Name two teachers she had in grade school.

42. Her typical day almost always includes:

_____ Doing a crossword

_____ Meditating

_____ Checking her horoscope

_____ Exercising

_____ Reading the news

_____ Calling and/or texting her best friend

43. Does she know how to play:

_____ Bridge? _____ Poker?

_____ Blackjack? _____ Go Fish?

44. Can she can tell the difference between Coke and Pepsi blindfolded?

_____ Yes _____ No

45. If you were offered a great job for two years a thousand miles away, would she go:

_____ Willingly? _____ Kicking and screaming?

_____ Reluctantly? _____ She wouldn't go.

46. Has she ever been stopped for speeding?

_____ Yes, once or twice

_____ Yes, more often than that

_____ Never

47. Does she have any photos or paintings of her grandparents or earlier ancestors?

_____ Yes, pictures of _____.

_____ No

48. Does she know:

_____ How many pints are in a quart?

_____ How to update her phone's operating system?

_____ What a Phillips screw looks like?

49. She's most likely to contribute volunteer time to which kind of charity?

_____ Religious _____ Child-related

_____ Environmental _____ Elderly-related

50. Has she ever dyed her hair an unusual color or painted her nails an unconventional shade?

____ Hair   ____ Nails

51. You're hiking with friends in an unfamiliar place and come to a sign: "Private Property." One friend says, "They're trying to stop hunters and campers, not us." Your bride says:

____ "That's right. Let's go ahead."

____ "'Private Property' means private property.
We shouldn't trespass."

____ (turning to you) "What do you think?"

52. As far as she's concerned, when a baby cries in a restaurant:

____ The parents should take the child outside or to another room.

____ Others in the room should lighten up and live with it.

53. Does she remember more or less than you do about the first time you met?

____ More   ____ About the same

____ Less

54. How does she like sleeveless T-shirts on men?

____ They're hot.   ____ They're OK.

____ On the right guy,   ____ She detests the look.
they're hot.

55. Can she touch her elbows together behind her back?

____ Yes   ____ No

56. Has she ever added a quart of oil to a car engine?

____ Yes   ____ No

57. Does she think dressing twins alike:

____ Is cute?   ____ Can do psychological

____ Is OK sometimes?   damage to the kids?

58. Would she like free lessons in:

____ Ballroom dancing?

____ Cabinet making?

____ Cake decorating?

____ Calligraphy?

59. Has she ever been an officer of a club or organization?

____ Yes: _____ _____

____ No

60. What's the longest she's ever talked on the phone in one session?

____ Less than an hour   ____ Two to four hours

____ One to two hours   ____ Longer than four hours

61. She thinks hanging around all day in pj's or a nightshirt, not once going out, is:

_____ Decadent, but a wonderful way to spend a day now and then.

_____ Perfectly fine any time.

_____ Something only losers do.

62. Which choices would she make?

_____ Dog	or	_____ Cat
_____ Pencil	or	_____ Pen
_____ Rock	or	_____ Rap
_____ Chocolate	or	_____ Vanilla
_____ Sunday in church	or	_____ Sunday at the beach

63. When she shops for clothes, does she look first to a particular:

_____ Store?   _____ Brand?

_____ Style?   _____ Color?

64. She thinks old-fashioned names for kids are:

_____ Cute   _____ Stuffy

_____ Solid and traditional   _____ Trendy

65. Has she ever lost a ring?

_____ Yes   _____ No

66. Which of her friends has a name she really likes?

67. Is there a foreign language she'd love to learn?

____ Yes: _____

____ No, she's satisfied with what she knows.

68. Has she ever laughed so hard that she peed her pants?

____ Once or twice   ____ So far, never

____ More than that   ____ Not that I know of...

69. What's her idea of comfort food?

70. Does she have a favorite comic strip?

____ Yes: _____

____ No

71. Does she think any of these should be legalized everywhere?

____ Marijuana   ____ Prostitution

____ Gambling   ____ Jaywalking

72. Which descriptions apply to her relationship with her parents?

_____ She's pretty good friends with her mother.

_____ Her mother disapproves of much of what she does.

_____ She's embarrassed to be seen with her mother.

_____ She and her father have a good relationship.

_____ She doesn't talk to her father all that much.

_____ She's always in conflict with her father about something.

73. If you could have your choice of plastic surgery, what work would she recommend that you have? Or would she want you to have nothing done at all?

74. Does she often read more than one book at a time?

_____ Yes, she goes back and forth as the mood strikes.

_____ No, she sticks with one until she's finished it.

75. "Men and women can never be just friends." Does your bride:

_____ Agree?   _____ Disagree?

76. Has she ever been:

_____ Really drunk?

_____ Lost in a parking lot?

_____ So happy or touched that she cried?

_____ Unable to stop laughing in a quiet public place?

77. Which friends, neighbors, or relatives, in her opinion, have raised spoiled brats?

78. Her ideal New Year's Eve would be:

_____ At home, with just the two of you?

_____ With a small group of friends or relatives?

_____ At a big party?

_____ In a giant, outdoor crowd?

79. When she's home alone, does she generally:

_____ Turn on the radio for background noise?

_____ Turn on the TV or a podcast?

_____ Play music?

_____ Enjoy the quiet?

80. How does your bride rank these qualities in a partner?

_____ Sex appeal   _____ Reliability

_____ Sense of humor   _____ Charm and politeness

_____ Smarts   _____ Kindness

81. Which of her married friends and relatives does she think found the all-around best husband?

82. If she were looking to get a dog, would she prefer one:

_____ From a breeder, to be sure of what she's getting?

_____ From a pound, to save the dog's life?

_____ From anywhere, as long as the dog is cute?

83. Does she think using foul language around a toddler:

_____ Is unwise, since kids pick up their behavior from adults?

_____ Is no big deal, since the kid's going to learn the words eventually?

_____ Can lead to some funny incidents, so the more the merrier?

84. Can she whistle:

_____ Any tune you name?   _____ Just a few faint tweets?

85. Does she believe the death penalty is justified:

____ For every murder conviction?

____ In certain rare circumstances?

____ In no case at all?

86. Which statements hit home with her?

____ "If records or books aren't in some kind of logical order, I go nuts."

____ "I cut all the food on my plate into bite-sized pieces before starting to eat."

____ "If the phone rings after ten o'clock at night, I jump."

____ "I can wrap a gift better than any store can."

____ "If a drawer or cupboard door is open, I close it."

87. When shopping for these staples, is she loyal to a single brand or does she shop by price or availability?

	LOYAL	NOT
SHAMPOO		
MAYONNAISE		
BEER OR SODA		
COFFEE OR TEA		
LAUNDRY DETERGENT		

88. Dogs and cats on the furniture? She thinks:

_____ If you want nice things, pets have to be taught
to stay on the floor.

_____ Pets are more important than chairs and sofas, so let 'em up.

_____ It depends on the pet.

89. She thinks people with gray hair:

_____ Should do something about it...quick.

_____ Shouldn't worry.

_____ Can be really sexy.

90. In which languages can she count to five?

91. The last time she bounced a payment?

_____ During the past month

_____ During the past year

_____ Can't remember—it was ages ago

_____ Never

92. How many rings does your bride ordinarily wear, anywhere on her body?

_____ None   _____ Two

_____ One   _____ Three or more

93. When did she last think seriously about a drastic hairstyle change?

_____ Within the past month   _____ More than a year ago

_____ Within the past year   _____ Never

94. Excluding family, who's the person your bride has counted as a friend the longest?

95. Does she know anyone with tattoos that are hidden by ordinary clothing?

_____ Yes: _____

_____ No one

96. How does she sign her name on a formal document? How does she plan to sign after she's married?

_____ Now: _____

_____ After marriage: _____